NORTHERN LIGHTS

POEMS

COLETTE WITTORSKI

Translated by

FRED JOHNSTON

Belfast
LAPWING

First Published by Lapwing Publications
c/o 1, Ballysillan Drive
Belfast BT14 8HQ
lapwing.poetry@ntlworld.com
http://www.freewebs.com/lapwingpoetry/

Since before 1632
The Greig sept of the MacGregor Clan
Has been printing and binding books

All Lapwing Publications are
Hand-printed and Hand-bound in Belfast
Set in Aldine 721 BT at the Winepress

ISBN 978-1-907276-06-4

CONTENTS

Colette Wittorski est née au Havre, un grand port de Normandie, avant la dernière guerre mondiale. Son père est d'origine lituanienne. Sa mère meurt à sa naissance. Réfugiée à la campagne avec sa famille pendant l'occupation allemande, elle poursuit ses études par correspondance.

Plus tard, elle fait une licence de philosophie. Le mémoire qu'elle soutient ensuite à la Sorbonne a pour titre : Philosophie et poésie. Le mythe chez Platon.

Suivent quelques années de travail à Paris dans l'édition puis dans l'enseignement. Elle tente de publier un premier recueil de poèmes et la lettre de refus de l'éditeur, pourtant relativement bienveillante, la blesse profondément. Elle se marie et se replie sur sa famille. Elle appartient à un milieu et une génération de femmes dont on n'attend pas qu'elles travaillent, et son mari ne l'encourage guère à écrire.

Il faudra le mouvement de mai 68 et une longue psychanalyse pour l'éveiller à elle-même. Fuyant l'éducation nationale, elle travaille comme animatrice, surtout dans un foyer de travailleurs maghrebins, puis comme formatrice dans les mêmes milieux. Désormais la poésie l'a rejointe et elle retrouve l'inspiration de sa jeunesse. En même temps elle se forme à Paris à diverses thérapies et devient psychothérapeute.

Elle vit maintenant en Centre Bretagne avec son compagnon, sculpteur et peintre, elle écrit toujours des poèmes.

Colette Wittorski was born in Le Havre, Normandy, before the second world war. Her father was of Lithuanian origin; her mother died while giving birth to Colette. Having fled to the countryside with her family during the German occupation, she continued her studies by correspondence course. Later she did a degree in philosophy. Her main dissertation at the Sorbonne was entitled : "Philosophy and Poetry. Myth in Plato."

There followed some years working in Paris in publishing and teaching. She tried to have a first collection of poems published and, despite its tone of kind encouragement, was deeply hurt by the editor's letter of rejection.

She married and withdrew to devote herself to her family. She belonged to a background and generation of women who were not expected to go out to work, and her husband did not encourage her to write.

It took the events of May 68 - coupled with extensive psychoanalysis - to bring about a re-awakening. Abandoning the state education system, she worked as a social worker, mainly within the framework of a hostel for North African workers, then in adult education within the same area. From now an poetry returned to her and she regained the inspiration of her youth. At the same time, she studied various therapies and became a psychotherapist.

She now lives in Central Brittany with partner, the sculptor and painter, Olivier Danican, and continues to write poetry.

¥

I discovered the poems of Colette Wittorski in a bookshop in Brittany amongst collections by local poets. I was at once taken by the immediacy and intimacy of the poems as I began draft-translating them while still in Brittany. Before long, I visited her at the converted farmhouse with its magnificent views which she shares with her husband, the eminent sculptor and onetime Résistance member, Olivier Danican, at Landeleau, Brittany. We viewed the marvellous sculptures, the paintings reflecting the earth and the natural world, while the sloping garden drew the eye downwards and across a plain. Here we discussed poetry and how I might attempt to translate some of her work.

The two collections from which poems are represented here are Une aurore boréale, published in 2006 by Editions an Amzer in 2006, and Un Bouquet de corde, published in 2003 from Librairie-Galerie Racine. The former took the Grand Prix an Amzer in 2005.

Interestingly, the Breton word 'amzer' can mean weather as well as another meaning of the French word, *les règles*, the two if taken with a pinch of imagination indicating both a feminine principle and the notion of changing and altering seasons. *Jardin sans lieu* and *Éclats d'ombre* have since appeared from JMG Création at Le Faou.

I am deeply indebted to Daphne Hassett, whose advice and direction on translation was inestimable and who is also a long-time friend of the poet and was thus able to interpret for me the meanings behind the meanings. Any translation errors are my own.

It is no easy thing to translate another poet's work. Arguably, it is easier to translate prose than poetry. Each translated word is a piece in a jigsaw; eventually a picture emerges, but one is dogged always by the one piece that doesn't seem to fit, even when all possible pieces have been used.

This is when a leap of faith, or perhaps poetic imagination, is the only viable solution. Translating anything word-for-word is fine for drafts, but not suitable for an interpretation of the vagaries and unique characteristics of a thought and created language from one tongue to another. The poet-translator makes this leap in full knowledge of the chasm beneath him and the depth to which he might fall; any attempt to delve into the original author's creative consciousness is bound to be fraught with serious difficulties. This is how translating from the original language is actual translating, a moving from one element to another, whereas working from supplied and already-translated cribs is not translating but interpreting; it's the difference between someone telling you where the troublesome jigsaw piece belongs and finding out for yourself.

Sometimes the piece also belongs to another picture: Daphne Hassett's suggestion of a children's song, and my thinking lines from it might explain the nuances of lines in Poem 3 of Wittorski's 'Origines', is a case in point. The imagistic richness of Wittorski's work, and the style of its being laid down, is different from what contemporary Irish poetry – in English or Irish – is familiar with.

It is, like so much European poetry, intensely visual and likely to produce images and emotions which startle us; thus we translate again, trying to get to what she means. Some poems do echo events or recollections in the poet's life; others tend towards a more lyrical nostalgic quality. Some are touching, others thought-provoking. Her poetic-thematic reach is considerable; she can project her thought into the shattered streets of Baghdad ('Bagdad' in French) with the same intensity as she can describe the tensions between her parents. And yet, though the personal seldom deserts the poems, she is never self-indulgent.

One hesitates to suggest how these poems are to be read by the readership of a country which neither anticipated nor experienced any of the influential European literary 'movements' and from which so many writers fled, seeking fresh creative air. Reading Kavanagh or Clarke in order to access Wittorski's poetry won't do. 'Modernist' poetry (one uses the term non-specifically) never reached Ireland and those who wished, like Brian Coffey for instance, (a Catholic-rooted writer and a philosopher) to write differently, out of the mould, moved to France in the early 'Thirties: Thomas MacGreevy and Denis Devlin were also there, and they in turn sought out Samuel Beckett. Even when Brian Coffey returned to London in the 'Fifties, he continued to write and publish in French; ironically, he confirmed himself as an Irish Modernist with his translations of Mallarmé. In terms of prose, one is taken by how the work of, say, Alain Robbe-Grillet has no contemporary reflection in Britain or Ireland; in terms of painting, Impressionism is a strictly French invention. The notion of, for want of a better word, experimentation, seems to be more common in French literature, where there is often little fracture between philosophy and literature and where a more holistic approach is offered to the arts in general: it is not uncommon, in fact it is virtually a rule, that the lowliest French poetry magazine will frequently contain articles discussing painting or cinema or music; Robbe-Grillet was also a film-maker.

Arguably, neither England nor Ireland could have produced a Baudelaire, with his acutely visual, actual, flâneurisme.

He gave birth to a form of Romanticism as an antidote to the ravages, social and imaginative, of the Industrial revolution; the latter to a romanticism based on myth and based in nationalism.

The French did not undergo an Industrial Revolution as we understand the term and the Revolution and the Terror were already undergoing serious revision when Baudelaire first translated Edgar Allen Poe. Thereafter French art and letters strove to redefine themselves in terms of the imaginative reinterpretation of the ordinary and the real and this was a quite deliberate striving, which flirted with a Romanticism from which some elements of French poet are not yet cured. Nor was 19th century French poetry concerned with defining a sense of nationalism, as was the case in Ireland.

The excellent contemporary Irish poet, Maurice Scully, with a few others, continues to hold and relight a Modernist poetry torch but, significantly, is drowned out by the persistent clamour of more conventional Irish poetry, which hasn't recovered from the marriage of Kavanagh and Clarke. There is a philosophical trend in Wittorski's work which is foreign too to Irish lyrical sensibilities. Now a deal of modern French poetry suffers from stylistic constriction and conservatism, as does our own. All is not imbued imagistic flair and the philosophy of the metaphor. Yet one should read these poems with an open imagination. One should sip at them and acclimatise one's palate to their newness and their flair. One should see them.

¥

Fred Johnston was born in Belfast in 1951 and has been a journalist and reviewer for many years. In 1986 he founded Galway City's annual literature festival, Cúirt – in the mid-Seventies, with Neil Jordan and Peter Sheridan, he had set up the Irish Writers' Co-operative. A novelist, critic and poet, he has recently begun to write poetry almost exclusively in French and to publish in France. He lives in Galway where he established The Western Writers' Centre (www.twwc.ie)

POEMS

1.

Ce soir le silence ne m'aime pas
La pointe du cristal qui dessine mes traces
Peine sur le limon
Et le vent les efface
Si bref est l'instant

Hâte-toi
Tire la corde inéluctable

Je voudrais tant
Prendre à l'aigle sa couronne
Et m'envoler

Colette Wittorski

2.

Tonight silence is no friend
a nib of rock-crystal hardly scratches the silt
and maps my tracks

and the breeze erases them
The moment is so brief
Make haste
stretch the fatal rope

I want so much
to take the crown from the eagle
and fly away

3.

Chacun relié
Accordé
Le présent prend sa place

Imperceptiblement les arbres
Se saluent dans leur forêt
Nous inclinons nos cimes

L'échange des bouquets
Nos voix si singulières
Coulent de source

4.

Each of us is connected
in harmony
The present takes its place

faintly the trees
nod at each other in their forest
we bow our heads

an exchange of flowers
our voices so strange
flow in the spring

5.

Hors des mots
Rouge torero la liane
Pend du chapiteau

L'insolence
Défie le dieu

Mais la nécessité sa suivante
Rôde dans les coulisses

6.

Beyond words,
the creeper, bullfighter-red
hangs from the capital

insolence mocks the god

but necessity, following him,
prowls behind the scenes

7.

Au coin du bois
Le dieu
Au coin de moi

8.

In a corner of the wood
the god
within me

9.

À la fourche de l'arbre

L'écartement se creuse

Pourtant
Confondue dans la foule
Avide
Elle boit le lait des jours

Et quand sa vie s'achève
Par les fentes du coeur
La ruche se vide

10.

In the fork of a tree
a fault-line opens

Nonethless
Smothered in the crowd
Greedily
She drains the milk of days

and when her life ends
From these cracks in the heart
The hive empties

11.

La guerre

Les morts seuls immobiles
Prévoir les rites funéraires

Ma chair se lève et danse
Les collines sautent sous leurs peaux de bête
Roses et bleus des champs d'herbes
Chavirent dans ma tête

Le terre a bu le sang

Ecarter le deuil
Tourner la clef du temps

12.

War

The dead alone don't move
arranging funerals

My flesh jumps and dances
hills leaping under their animal pelts
pastures of blue and red
somersault in my head

the fields have drunk blood
dispense with grief
to turn time's key

13.

Vieillesse

C'est la fonte des glaces
Et sur le sol qui bouge
La menace de l'engloutissement

Chacun fuit
Les rires se taisent
Le lac se vide

14.

Old Age

is ice melting
and on the altering earth
the threat of being swallowed

we flee
the lake runs out
laughter becomes silence

15.

Ta bouche était une arche de lumière vibrante

Je suis entrée

Et les vagues de tout l'océan
Inséparable
Ont pénétré mon sang

Ce fut à coeur ouvert
Douce lame de ton épée
Dont le feu rythme mon soleil

Pour la traversée

16.

Your mouth an arc of living light

I entered

And the waves of the world's ocean
In a surge
Flowed into my blood

My heart opened
To the sweet blade of your sword
Whose fire pulsed in time to my sun

On its sky-voyaging

17.

Ecrire le monde
Donner les mots

Et le seuil de soie
Sous mon pied nu
Crée l'élan

D'oser seule entrer
Au coeur

18.

To write the world
to offer words

the silken threshold
beneath my bare feet
lends a surge

of courage
to cut, alone, straight
to the heart

19.

Ecorchée vive mon âme
Et le vent l'intercepte
Il souffle sur mes fleurs de peau
Et les viole

20.

My soul is flayed
and the wind grabs at it
it breathes on my senses
and violates them

21.

Je n'ai pas vu l'éclair de la dague
J'ignore le lieu de ma blessure
Et l'ampleur des dégâts
Je suis Bagdad en feu
Brûlant dans ma mémoire
Je hurle de douleur

22.

I didn't catch the flash of bladed light
I can't see where I've been wounded
nor the extent of the damage
I am Baghdad burning
blazing in my remembering
I scream in pain

23.

L'acrobate se balance

Au fil du temps
Au fil du sang
A la corde du coeur

Pour le recevoir
Parfois
Le filet des douleurs

24.

The acrobat balances
on time's wire
a string of heart's blood

to catch him
now and then
the net of pain

25.

'Ouvre les yeux
Le jour m'attend
Déjà les oiseaux vibrent de leurs chants

Posé plus bas
Sur d'autres cimes
Un lac de brume passagère
Masque le torrent

Et me transmet ses certitudes

26.

I open my eyes
the day waits
Already birds thrill the air with song

Set below
between other peaks
a lake of shifting fog
obscures the mountain stream

mirrors back to me its certainties

27.

Errant entre les familles
Bousculée par les espèces
Pressée stressée usée
Enfin je joins le temps des arbres
Et mêle à la leur ma lenteur

28.

Wandering among families
banged about by their own
pressured stressed broken
at last I make it back to the rhythm of trees
and mingle my slow pace with theirs.

29.

Dormeurs parallèles

Creusant dans l'eau du temps
Leurs traces éphémères
Nageurs de mes songes
Ils furent mes parents

Le cataclysme vint

Désormais séparés
Gelée morte ma mère
Et lui glacé vivant
Dans un lac sombre
Comme un ventre de sang
Tirant de moi son feu
Il fut un survivant

30.

Two sleepers side-by-side,
delving deep in the water of time
their wakes blurry
swimmers in my dreams
such were my parents

disaster struck

separated forevermore
my mother icily dead
and he frozen alive
in a black lake
like a wombful of blood
drawing his fire from me
he was a survivor

31.

Origines

1

Les dieux secouèrent les dés
Et mon destin tomba
Masqué le grand hasard
Agitait ses sonnettes
Quand les chevaux de mon nom
Intraduisible
L'inscrivirent dans leur galop

32

Origins

1

the gods play dice
and my destiny tumbles out
sly chance rings its bells
as the horses engrave in their gallop
my illegible name

2

Oh ma jument ma belle
La première qui m'allaita
Debout déjà
La tête contre ton ventre

Sur la colline nacrée
Tu m'apprenais chaque matin
A saluer le grand cerf de lumière
Déployant ses cornes d'arbre
A l'horizon sanglant

Car le couteau passa

2

O my young mare my beauty
the first to suckle me
standing already
your head on your breast

On the pearly hill
you taught me each morning
to bow to the proud stag of pure light
opening its horns of trees
to the blood-red horizon

for the knife calls

3

Désormais
Dans la pénombre des humains
Aladin est parti
En emportant la lampe
Nous n'irons plus au bois.*
Les têtes sont coupées

Même nos âmes se sont enfuies

Line recalling a well-known old children's song

3

From now on
in humanity's twilight
Aladdin has left
taking his lamp with him

We'll go no more to the woods.
The laurels are cut down

even our souls have fled

Northern Lights

NOTES

*These lines are taken from the opening verse of the children's dance-song, *Nous N'irons plus au Bois,* a theme taken up by Debussy in his *Les Jardins sous la pluie.*

"Nous n'irons plus au bois
Les lauriers sont coupés,
La belle que voila
Ira les ramasser . . ."

I am sincerely grateful for comments by Anne-Marie Glasheen and for pointing to Theodore de Banville's *Nous n'irons plus au bois,*

"Nous n'irons plus au bois, les lauriers sont coupés.
Les amours des bassins, les Naiades en groupe
Voient reluier au soleil . . . ."

and even to A.E.Housman's *We'll go to the woods no more,*

"We'll go to the woods no more.
The laurels are all cut . . . ."

It is probably safe to say that the folk-song came first and the symbol is very old; the proliferation of the symbolism is interesting, when one considers the late Kathleen Raine's belief that true poets thought in symbolic language or had knowledge of it. In Book 1 of Ovid's *Metamorphoses,* Daphne becomes a laurel so that she may not marry Apollo; in France the laurel is represented in the title of the examination, 'Baccalaureate,' laurels being the bay leaf, or 'bacca lauri,' indicating the involvement of Bacchus, the God of Wine and therefore a sort of enlightenment; in representations of Apollo, the god carries a branch or sprig of laurels; the Muse Clio was the goddess of epic poetry and of history – poetry thus being linked to the notion of a versed form of retelling tribal lineage – and wore laurels in her hair; see also Milton's use of the laurel as poetic symbol; the leaves of the sweet bay, or 'poet's laurel,' are used in cooking; in song, it crops up in *Green Grows the Laurel*, and arguably it is this song, popular in the Spanish-American War, which produced the pejorative, 'gringo,' from 'Green Grow . . .'; the green laurel is thought by singer Len Graham to be symbolic of young love and fickleness and was also a symbol of Irish political loyalty.

Apollo loved – or at least lusted after - Daphne, so it's natural that, when she became a laurel tree, he should make the laurel his favourite; but clearly the symbol of the laurel is enlightenment in all senses; courage, learning, self-awareness, and awakening love. Cutting down the laurel therefore heralds a spiritual and psychical darkening; both Housman's poem and and de Banville's reflect this, the absence of the thriving laurel a symbol of loss and abandonment, even land – or the soul – laid waste: "even our souls have fled" says Wittorski.

In the children's song, the girl collecting them is probably Daphne who, having 'lost' the foliage of her disguise, is now in danger from Apollo.

Thus the cutting down of the laurels represents the loss of innocence and even the plunder of innocence in an unwished-for way and at the same time is symbolic of a rite-of-passage from childhood into adulthood.